# THE OBSERVER EFFECT

*poems*

**K. M. LIGHTHOUSE**

Copyright © 2018 by K. M. Lighthouse
All rights reserved.

Published in the United States
Portland, Oregon

A version of "The Stories Walls Tell Don't Change," previously called "Three Days," appeared first in *Mapping Salt Lake City*, and "Habitual Loneliness" was previously published by *Blue Lake Review*.

Paperback ISBN: 978-0-9972987-4-1

Book cover & typography by Ash Good
www.ashgood.design

# THE OBSERVER EFFECT

*poems*

| | |
|---|---|
| 9 | People Watching on the Threshold of Before and After |
| 10 | The Stories Walls Tell Don't Change |
| 12 | Octopus Paella |
| 15 | The Great Poet |
| 17 | He Would Smoke American Spirits |
| 19 | Accident |
| 20 | Public Service Announcement |
| 23 | Theatrics |
| 25 | Dust to Dust |
| 27 | As an Adult, He Plants from Seed |
| 28 | Later, He Tells Her Even Orange Peels Are Commodities |

| | |
|---|---|
| 30 | Calder |
| 31 | Habitual Loneliness |
| 33 | Alone at a Table for Six |
| 34 | In the Morning, She Remembers Everything |
| 35 | Those Pans She Got for Christmas? She's Putting Them to Good Use |
| 36 | Shirk |
| 37 | I Am the Man |
| 39 | Instead of a Spotlight, a Movie Fragment |
| 40 | When the Stage Is Level with General Admission |
| 41 | Abstraction |
| 42 | We Watch Again in Memory of Ourselves |

"The observer, when he seems to himself to be observing a stone, is really, if physics is to be believed, observing the effects of the stone upon himself."

—BERTRAND RUSSELL

## *People Watching on the Threshold of Before and After*

The woman outside
Pappaccino's paces in the rain,

Bluetooth headset glowing
to match the purpose in her pencil skirt.

From behind the glass, we imagine
who she is while she mouths swallowed syllables.

She's not wearing shoes warm enough
to walk in the rain,

and maybe her stomach grumbles at well-past lunch,
her feet blister and hair lazily uncurls,

her body born worn.
We remember that conception

doesn't happen in a fit of passion but happens
up to 12 hours later at the grocery store,

on a bus, during sex
with another man — never mind who the father is —

and we wonder if it will happen here while we watch
this woman pace in front of glass in the rain.

## The Stories Walls Tell Don't Change

After the remodel, she's in the hospital again,
one of eight large municipal hospitals
in Salt Lake City;

she can count them on her fingers:
LDS, St. Marks, University, Regional . . .
How could she forget? It's the smell of antiseptic.

They say smell is strongly tied to memory
so when she's here and her brother dies again,
she shouldn't be surprised.

We ask if we should get a chaplain
before we pull the plug.
Can you grieve for someone after knowing him

three days? Her father punches a hole in the wall,
but the maintenance crew patch it
12 minutes later.

She wanted to be at home when her brother died,
and maybe that's why he still lives here
and in the apartment next door

where an infant cries in darkness. He lives
in his own absence,
even when this hospital

is as unrecognizable as her family
post-mortem.
*We want to make everyone comfortable . . .*

Fifty-seven percent of deaths occur in hospitals,
and still, we remind her,
*. . . family members die here.*

## Octopus Paella

The octopus, when it arrives, sits
with a vacancy in its eyes, which peek above the water
in the bucket. The five-gallon bucket—
grimy, once-white—is a poor excuse
of a container for such intelligence at $125 an entrée.

In a flat voice, someone mentions
their cousin who, in Italy, saw live octopus roll around
in a modified concrete mixer until dead, and how, on a fishing trip,
the guide speared an octopus, pulled its body
inside out, and fed intestines to surrounding fish.

The station chef stares blankly as tentacles reach
around the metal handle and survey the room.
When he turns and forces
his head past peripheral vision, he can still hear
sucking tentacles slop against plastic.

We back away, so he knows we have decided.
It could only ever have been him. Him, stoic
in the ways of beast and vegetable, fire
of the kitchen, angry enough to murder a man with his voice.
*Put it on the table*, we say. *Cover it in salt.*

*We don't want it to get tough.* Now, the trick:
keep fear out of its muscles. Pound the fear out
in favor of compliance and taste. Pound it with this
heavy club of a meat tenderizer.
What choice is there? We are watching.

Salt—rubbed on quick in thick strokes—and drying bucket water
makes his hands stick to flesh. He tries
to turn his head again, but his eyes cannot unfix themselves,
stuck on suckers as if they themselves were pupils and irises
reflecting his image.

*More salt.* More salt. If the tiny monster had a human mouth,
maybe it would scream. But maybe
it would continue to hold composure, relaxed
in the beating to soften even the blows.
*Hold it down. Keep it there.*

The tenderizer feels awkward, unbalanced, weighty,
heavy-handed.
*Keep it alive, we say. Make it soft.*
Hand raises, heavy from blunt weapon, and down
down             down, slam flesh between metal table

and metal hammer, and again,
up        down            up
down, and time moves with bodies, speeding up
and slowing
down in rhythm, itself wincing at the blows.

And it has been years in a matter of seconds, seconds
in a matter of hours. How long have we stared eyes into eyes?
A tentacle curls around a left hand, but that tentacle is next.
Fingers pry suckers from skin, each with a sickening *shol-lunk*,
still moist with bucket water and sweat—the tears of the body.

The kitchen doesn't resume. We glance
at the spectacle with peripheral stares of shame and collective ruin.
The creature doesn't run but sees us,
eyes somehow growing wider with not fear or anguish or anger—
pity. Stomach sick with the seawater churning within, arms cling

to the metallic table, sticky now with bucket-watered blood.
Eyes still stare — up
down      up        down      up        down
up —
An hour and a half.

It takes an hour and a half to murder
an octopus for two bowls of paella.
When bodies slump down and the weapon clatters,
hands, fingers, tentacles
still maintain the curled form required for beating.

This rigidity, to reasonable a price
for life.

## The Great Poet

We knew a poet once. Or, rather,
we knew of her. She locks
her breaths away where no one can find them,
as if, by knowing that she is alive somewhere,

her audience might take a piece of her.
Broken shards of opaque glass
fill her lungs
in place of air—naked,

raw slivers of creation she alone wants to own
but can never copy right.
When she reads her work, we see all of it
at once, buried underneath her descriptions

of the knolls on a tree, concealed
in the way she tells us the airplane
gives her mother wings,
secreted in the all-too-natural hues

she remembers
from Thailand. She speaks of ghosts
and wraiths
as if she were not one.

*Everything dies*, she says.

She sees our eyes and knows—
though we stand across
the room—that we, too, write,
even as her bangs, in three black curls, fall

in front of her face like bars
of a cell.
Her writing should inspire ours,
and yet, she steals

the inspiration we do not yet have,
words we never put down to paper.
She empties us, and the void
makes us all hungry. Taking out a pencil, we scribble

her lines as she speaks them, sickened
that we cannot write anything else. The page fills
as our thoughts try to blot out her rhymes,
metaphors, alliterations.

*Everything dies,* the poet says.

Yes, everything dies, like her beautiful words
filtered through plastic and ink, default
fonts and computer screens, the eyes
of published critics, rewritten here

as if they were ours.
*Everything dies,* the great poet says.

*He Would Smoke American Spirits*

Our graduate student professor, the short one
with the squeaky voice, had toilet-bowl dreams
of fucking Ronald Reagan in hell
and warned us
of lesser-known STDs like music and cigarettes.

He never smoked one, but he's addicted.
There's something romantic
about slow lung death
and socially acceptable ways to take years off
your life — minute-by-minute suicide,

neatly packaged in rows.
Dad asked him to bring two packs
of Marlboro 100 Smooths
to Newport, and if it weren't for plastic wrap,
Dad wouldn't have noticed one missing,

manic-drunk and pain-high.
Hell, he could have done it anyway
or gone to any convenience store,
but the clerks speak
with our professor's voice.

Instead, he smokes from bongs
he never gets the hang of, coughing and paranoid
while he writes in all caps and hopes his future
self believes him, that drugs are not enough
to blame the crazy on. It's only a little

harder to disregard himself
when he's sober.

*Accident*

We giggle drunkenly
with apology,
having walked into her unlocked
bathroom stall
and stared at her uneven
posture,
at fallen lips spread wide, at knees
that scream of scars
and too much screentime.

Maybe she should move,
flinch,
cover herself.
But, no, she just waits.
Five, ten, fifteen, an hour
to regain dignity
in the comfort of strangers
who know nothing
but clothes.

## Public Service Announcement

Don't use public bathrooms unless there is no other option.
    If you must use them, only use them to urinate.
Never call a bathroom anything that relates to its actual use. Avoid words such as "toilet" and instead refer to non-existent baths.
Upon entering a public bathroom:
    Don't make eye contact.
        If you do make eye contact, act embarrassed and look away immediately.
    Don't use a stall next to another occupied stall.
        If there is a line for the bathroom, seek out another bathroom.
    Don't go in a stall someone just came out of.
It is inappropriate to make noises in the stalls.
If you must sit down, don't sigh or sound relieved.
If you must undress yourself, don't unzip your pants loudly or let your belt clink together.
If you must urinate, cough and simultaneously pull out toilet paper to mask the sound.
If you must unwrap a tampon or pad, use the same procedure you use for urination.
If you must loose your stool, don't let it splash.
If you must pass gas, make sure you are the only one in the bathroom, even if you must peek into other stalls to be certain.
Don't touch anything in a public bathroom.
    Touch bathroom items only if the following conditions exist:
        The entrance door isn't automated.
        The stall door isn't automated.
        The lock on the stall door isn't automated.
        The toilet seat cover dispenser isn't automated.
        The flushing mechanism isn't automated.
        The toilet paper roll isn't automated.

    The garbage can lid isn't automated.
    The sink isn't automated.
    The soap dispenser isn't automated.
    The hand dryer isn't automated.
    The paper towel dispenser isn't automated.
    The baby changing table isn't automated.
    The tampon dispenser isn't automated.

If you must be on your period while using a public bathroom, adhere to the following:

    Never visibly carry your pad or tampon into the bathroom.
    Never use the tampon and pad dispensers; they are empty to remind you not to use them.
    Never drip any blood on the toilet seat.
    Never accidentally bleed on your pants or underwear because you waited to use the bathroom.
    Never wrap your used tampon or pad in fewer than 12 toilet paper sheets.

When there are other people in the bathroom, make sure everyone hears and sees you practicing good hygiene. You can do this by adhering to these suggestions:

    Make unnecessary noise while pulling out and putting on the disposable toilet seat cover.
    If there are not any disposable toilet seat covers, bring your own or complain about their absence.
    Wash your hands one sink away from someone else who is already washing her hands.
    Use too much soap.
    Scrub your hands vigorously for one and half minutes.
        If you wash your hands for any longer, other bathroom users will assume you have OCD.

Use a paper towel, toilet paper, or a tissue to turn on the faucet and open the door (if they aren't automated).

If you must use the bathroom for unconventional or questionable activities such as drinking, having sex, throwing up, crying, smoking, masturbating, doing drugs, giving blow jobs, or changing clothes (see the public service announcement for locker rooms), please follow these customary rules:

Keep arms and legs inside the stall at all times.

Make sure that no one will see body parts, clothes, shoes, bags, or anything else from inside the neighboring stall(s).

Never allow your head above or below the stall walls.

Keep noises to a minimum.

Reduce smells if at all possible.

Wait until everyone has left the bathroom before coming out.

This has been a public service announcement for the good of all women who use public bathrooms. If you have questions, comments, or concerns about how to adhere to these straightforward rules, please contact the janitorial staff at the establishment nearest you.

## *Theatrics*

At nine years old, he finds her in the bathtub.
*She slipped*, we tell him, but what cuts from wrists
to antecubitals to shoulders?
That night, his purple shower curtain grows darker
with the violet blossoms of her,

the water so saturated he can't remember it colorless.
Her attacker goes unknown,
and his imageless, handwritten wanted posters
do nothing but elicit glazed stares from distant relatives.
To feign belief, he lays mats to prevent future slips, plasters

every bathroom in the house.
In later weeks, he stops washing,
the dread more abhorrent than self-sustained stench.
The smell of the toilet begins to curdle
into the familiarity

of diluted blood, full of iron
and rust and rinse-cycle raindrops.
Public restrooms beget the aroma
of mass graves, the white tile a waiting canvas.
Bathtubs fill the buildings of his dreams, fill living rooms

with death
and knife-sharp faucets. In bathrooms,
his breath remains shallow like drying puddles,
his lungs punctured rafts.
And then the reality of her would not be contained

in bathrooms but burst forth in floods
to kitchen sinks, drinking fountains, cold beverage aisles.
Wet floor signs warn him like crosses on sides of roads—
they, too, are lies—and everywhere speaks of secret deaths.
He does not dare to cry because the water lives

within, too, and by then, inevitability
overcomes him in deep shades of fresh bruises
and warm blood as he lays starfished
on his sister's bathroom floor and screams, *Come get me!*
before we tell him he must be sleepwalking again.

*Dust to Dust*

Mother closes the net
and brandishes the bunched mesh.
The autumnal orange on muted
brown draws fingers in
while Mother cautions: *Don't
touch the butterfly dust,
or she'll forget to fly.*

She pulls her hand back and asks,
*Am I covered in butterfly dust?*
Mother laughs but says,
*Yes, so don't let strangers
touch you.*
She knows the two of them are
the butterfly's strangers.

She inspects her skin
for powdery butterfly scales
and wonders if that's where her color
comes from,
and perhaps, rubbing deeper than that,
she would become translucent,
her skin cracked and torn

like the crinkled insect exoskeletons
on her window sill.
When the school year returns,
the long-sleeved shirts in her closet
multiply—hanging like empty cocoons.
We older girls show off
shaved legs, bare of gold-

brown fuzz, and she imagines,
if the dust is anywhere,
it's in our hair.
She asks us, *who touched you?*
She asks if we remember to fly.
And arranged in orderly rows
of desks, we match

butterflies pinned under glass,
stiff in pretty appeasement—
the neat lines of names read the same:
Monarch, Peacock, Lady, Swallowtail;
Monique, Patricia, Lacy, Sharon.
Everyone begins to look like strangers—
her brother sprouts thick, black hairs

the color of necrosis; Mother
grays like dirty snow.
At dinner, she keeps her hands
in her lap; She runs from Auntie's kisses
and Grandpa's bristly hugs.
As dust settles
on the shelves of untouched limbs,

she is still forgetting to fly,
or perhaps she never flew at all.

## As an Adult, He Plants from Seed


The gardens of his childhood
were stillborn,
commercial-sized garbage bags of weeds
and raised beds, overgrown with pests

and rotted, rooting deeper
during barren winters
when we dared each other to eat
carrots three years late.

Now, he gardens in prisons where caging
tomatoes is a male privilege,
and the women's facility only plants flowers.
Now, he stands out in soggy boots

that couldn't make it
through Portland's wet winters.
Now, he pays $14.99 for a balcony rail planter
and $0.99 for a makeshift watering can

that's really a jug of distilled water
with holes in the top.
He plants free chamomile seeds
from the CBD booth at the farmer's market

in a quarter inch of soil and is surprised
when they poke out with pinhead leaves.
If he hadn't planted them himself,
he would have thought they were weeds.

### *Later, He Tells Her Even Orange Peels Are Commodities*

She has to wait for her father to call her.
It's his birthday, and she wrote letters

but hasn't bothered to send them.
She wants to ask if his hands

still strum imaginary guitar chords,
if there is an album in the making

behind bars.
What would those songs be called?

"Two Hours When I Disappeared
from the Walmart Parking Lot"

and "I Tipped the Waitress $200
so I Could Drink Outside"?

She'd need the whole album
for context.

His prelude tracks
consist of dial tones from payphones

in Fort Collins and the sound
of slumping to sleep against the cold cement

of a Catholic Church with his name.
Would he record "15-minute Prison Phone Call"

or "The Week No One Told Me
about the Vacation to Alaska"?

She might search for herself on that album
as much as he searches for himself

in her poems.
They find themselves everywhere.

## Calder

There's insanity in being the only one
who remembers,
and the ground no longer replies to her
as it did when her feet knew the dirt.
Maybe she had no place in coming back

to show off the blackened mold of a trailer home.
The gray sands of the riverbank
have eaten at the floorboards in mockery
of her memory;

she assumed he left more behind.
The creases on his face left
no imprint—
the boarded doors give no impression of him.
Maybe she had no right to bring us here

and there's no use sharing these memories.
After all, she's become an adult
now the evidence of her childhood
is dead.

*Habitual Loneliness*


There's nothing quite like loneliness.
It's not a feeling,
but a series of actions.
Loneliness is the urge to trim his toenails
so he might delay
going alone to bed a while longer.
Loneliness is checking a locked door
repeatedly

so he might hear the turn of a key.
Every step he takes includes a pause—
A listening for a break in silence.
He waits until the bathwater has gone cold
before draining it
and sits until the tub is dry—
staring.
He keeps only one light on at a time.

In the shadows, he could mistake
the unmade bed for a form, snuggled
tightly in wait for something warmer.
Light always corrects him, so his finger
lingers on the switch, and everything
takes a moment longer.
We imagine that this is why people slow
with age—loneliness

becomes habitual.
Bones wear from the pausing;
joints shrivel beyond repair.
And, a loved one's death
is just more permanent.
Just a time when no one walks
through the door, no one
turns the key,

and the body that's left refuses
to speed up.

## *Alone at a Table for Six*

He remembers being here
or a place like here
with lacquered wooden tables
and servers who fill glasses before
they go empty.

We are backdrop for the days
that drop off him and cascade
to the floor in the meekest of revolutions,
but then again, we also come to lose
ourselves in the cloth

of existence. All these places look like this:
blue-white lights to make him translucent,
stools with legs taller than his, graffitied
mirrors, lazy attempts at intimacy
in booth corners.

At least he's alone this time,
free of the scrutiny he's received before.
And what then when he has more in common
with street lamps
than those across the table?

What then except to crumple
inward with personal oblivion?
After all, it's a feeling he knows well,
so well, he met it at the bar
even before he arrived.

## In the Morning, She Remembers Everything

She drinks six different beers
at high altitude to prove she can,
and words she meant not to say
roll off her tongue in waves

like the nausea she pushes down
with more water.
*Do we want to keep doing this?*
she asks.

He hasn't had as much
as she has, and he lives here. In answer,
he throws all the spoons in the drawer
over the counter in playful arcs.

Though they've all touched the floor,
they put them back dirty,
a secret, tiny lie
for us, though they eat

with them, too, later.
She takes half-naked selfies in front of him,
and he puts on *Cloud Atlas*
after she has her contacts out.

It's three hours long,
and they only make it halfway,
though we told them the movie is better
than the book.

## *Those Pans She Got for Christmas? She's Putting Them to Good Use*

She feels she betrays her sex
when the most exciting part of her day
is his return from work

when he says his coworkers asked,
*what smelled so good?*
He'd say, *spaghetti squash burrito bowls*

or *Thai wonton cups with chive flowers.*
He'll tell them his wife made it.
So her meals become more elaborate;

she jumps cross-culturally across time
to learn skills she had only borrowed
before she was *wife*, before

she was *lover.*
And when she brings her own food
to work, there is no one to ask who made it.

## Shirk

All that's left of our grandmother
is a sewing machine,

and our mother only exists
in the seams of her clothes that remain intact—

How do we exist?
There are no stitches holding us here;

the biological craftsmanship
that came with us out of the womb

has withered away, being
more organic.

But, if we still exist, can we exist together?
The needle threatens us

and pierces fingers as if jealous
of the careful knitting of bone

and flesh.
We don't need thread;

I'll get the glue.

## *I Am the Man*

I am the man who hit him. I am the man who forced his face to hit the pavement at forty miles an hour — the curb now red; you can't park here. I am the man who ran. I am the man who went home in tears to a wife he could not tell, to children who haven't spoken to him since he started working late. I am the man who turns the news off because he knows what he will find there. I am the man who wishes he did not wake to the sound of a shattering skull on the windshield. I am the man who wants to turn back time exactly two days, six hours, 12 minutes, and seven — eight, nine — seconds to when he revved the gas in a desperate attempt to escape himself. I am the man who has a family to think about. I am the man who is afraid of the television, the radio, the conversations around the water cooler. I am the man who imagines it was his own skull, *his* left eye skittering across the pavement. I am the man who won't stop drinking, not now, not after that's what started it all. I am the man who shakes his head at the bartender when he asks if we heard about the kid with his brains on the cement, young kid, only 17 by the looks of it, works for Willy on the weekends. I am the man who cannot stand to look at himself in the mirror. I am the man who cleaned the blood and other fluids off the windshield with a blank face and shoved the rags in the bottom of the neighbor's trash can. I am the man who has nightmares of Oscar the Grouch telling the police. I am the man who cannot bring himself to make love to the woman he married because her face begins to change, to take on the features of the kid — the consequences of the squelching thud playing across her pale skin as if she were a projection screen. I am the man who wishes he was the kid because tangible pain — or better yet, death — would be easier. I am the man who is afraid of his legacy. I am the man who can't go to sleep because that means waking up again. I am the man who gazes at his hands — both sides — and wonders how they have become murderer's hands. I am the man who knows he's chicken-shit scared of being chicken-shit scared of being a coward. I am the man who dreams the kid was one of his own. I am the man who allows a foreign smile to play across his face, his lips forming a misshapen frame around his teeth. I am the man who stares at his hands like weapons. I am the man who has begun to frighten his wife. I am the man who ties her down too tightly, who keeps going when she says "no, no really, I'm finished," who keeps moving through her tears. I am the man who spends his work day sitting in the parking lot because it's been days since he's been in the office. I am the man with coworkers who think he's dead. I am the man who wishes it were true. I am the man who looks up facial reconstruction surgery to see if the kid's recovery is possible. I am the man who watches videos of vehicular manslaughter. I am the man who—goddammit—could not stop his hand as it begins to move up and down on his own penis. I am the man who cried because it felt better to know he was an even bigger piece of shit. I am the man who now spends the nights driving around the neighborhood where it happened. I am the man who sees the kid walking and veers to hit him again, only to wake up with his car smashed against a tree. I am the man who panics at the damage and sound and drives away from the scene again. I am the man who stops his car—some of its skull now missing—on the side of the freeway. I am the man who could make a man out of another man. I am the man who takes a breath and turns his lights off—light, now, since one has stopped working completely. I am the man who stares intently at the solid white line on the side of the road, gaze drifting toward the broken yellow. I am the man who sees fate as a pair of headlights—a semi, perfect. I am the man who turned himself into a squelching thud, an unrecognizable smear on the pavement. I am the man who gave another man the chance to stop.

## *Instead of a Spotlight, a Movie Fragment*

Sometimes, we have trouble existing.
It's the old tree-falling-in-a-forest metaphor,
the opposite of
solipsism.
This is us leaving impressions
on bus seats.

Proof could prove anything;
it's contaminated.
We live instead on a plane
of non-existence,
an infinity of disbelief. This is
the speed of water evaporating at room temperature.

This, our overture, is an absence
of sound.

## When the Stage Is Level with General Admission

Between skits, improv actors move
across an imagined set in patterns like fish
or furniture,

kaleidoscoping tessellation on stage
as they create in real time.
This is birth on display,

and we are the improv audience. Strings
above our heads move in unison, collective mirrors
for action.

We ribbon out until there is nothing
else to unfold,
until our complexities flatten

into sheets of creased origami paper,
once contorted but smooth now with lines
of practiced folding.

There aren't many of us, but
this paper quilt has so many colors.

*Abstraction*

The clicks of our heels
are cold echoes and reflections
of voices (asymmetrical, too,
like faces in mirrors).

This is a place where a person could cease
to exist—absorbed into
the meaning
of color and context.

In this place,
everything becomes ethereal—blurry
representations of selves
that stare at others' blood

laid out on stretched canvases.
In a museum,
we don't come to see the ghosts;
we come to become one—lost

in the prison of another's mind
that dwarfs the white walls.
Quiet footsteps speak this knowledge—
the hush that falls over us is an act

of recognition.
We are transitioning
to become a piece of artwork,
a block of color and line and shape.

## We Watch Again in Memory of Ourselves

We don't remember the womb,
don't remember the years before
we create and pass memory
to the analog "I"

where we are our own observers,
recording, translating, filtering our lives
into flipbook snapshots for future selves:
*this is important, this is not.*

And yet we forget this "I" is a copy
that becomes the original as we jolt and jerk
like cars with old transmissions
into remembered pasts and forget

we leave pieces behind. Not everything copies right;
instructions grow blurry, and — agency surrendered —
we lose ourselves for whole minutes
hours, days, years, sentences trailing off

before we stitch again souls into eyes
and remember we have no memory of death,
which means we are not just observers
and must still be alive.

**K. M. LIGHTHOUSE** graduated from the University of Utah and worked as the senior poetry director of *enormous rooms* for two years but has since made the Pacific Northwest a home. The poet's other works include publication in *Sonic Boom, From Sac, Blue Lake Review,* and *Mapping Salt Lake City* and a forthcoming chapbook entitled *you are an ambiguous pronoun.* K. M. Lighthouse is an assistant organizer with Portland's Eastside Poets and a member of High Priestesses of Poetry.

www.ingramcontent.com/pod-product-compliance
Lightning Source LLC
Chambersburg PA
CBHW070442010526
44118CB00014B/2155